TAILS from History

A Parrot in the Painting

THE STORY OF FRIDA KAHLO AND BONITO

By Thea Feldman

Illustrated by Rachel Sanson

Ready-to-Read

Simon Spotlight

New York   London   Toronto   Sydney   New Delhi

To Rose, who loves birds, too —T. F.

For my mum —R. S.

SIMON SPOTLIGHT
An imprint of Simon & Schuster Children's Publishing Division
1230 Avenue of the Americas, New York, New York 10020
This Simon Spotlight edition July 2018
Text copyright © 2018 by Simon & Schuster, Inc.
Illustrations copyright © 2018 by Rachel Sanson
For information about special discounts for bulk purchases, please contact
Simon & Schuster Special Sales at 1-866-506-1949 or business@simonandschuster.com.
Manufactured in the United States of America 0518 LAK
10 9 8 7 6 5 4 3 2 1
Library of Congress Cataloging-in-Publication Data
Names: Feldman, Thea, author. I Sanson, Rachel, illustrator. Title: A parrot in the
painting / by Thea Feldman ; illustrated by Rachel Sanson. Description: New York :
Simon Spotlight, [2018] I Series: Tails from history I Series: Ready-to-read I Audience:
Ages 5-7. Identifiers: LCCN 2017054384I ISBN 9781534422308 (hardcover)
ISBN 9781534422292 (pbk.) I ISBN 9781534422315 (eBook)
Subjects: LCSH: Kahlo, Frida—Juvenile literature. Painters—Mexico—Biography—
Juvenile literature. I Parrots in art—Juvenile literature. I Pets—Juvenile literature.
Classification: LCC ND259.K33 F45 2018 I DDC 759.972 [B]—dc23 LC record available
at https://lccn.loc.gov/2017054384

Squawk!

Bonito (say: boh-NEE-toh) the parrot
flapped his wings
and squawked loudly.

Bonito liked to squawk.
He had a lot to say!
He also liked to fly
around the garden
of the house where he lived.

The house was in Mexico.
It was called la Casa Azul
(say: lah KAH-sah ah-SOOL).
La Casa Azul means
"the Blue House" in Spanish.

A woman named Frida Kahlo
lived in the house.
She and her husband,
Diego Rivera, were painters.

Bonito wasn't the only animal
who lived there.
There were cats and dogs.
Some of the dogs had no hair!

There were
spider monkeys
who climbed trees
in the garden.

There was a pretty fawn
named Granizo
(say: grah-NEE-soh).

There were lots of
other birds besides
Bonito, too.

There were little parakeets
and big macaws.

There were chickens and
an eagle.
The chickens clucked and pecked
at food grains on the ground.

Frida painted
some of these animals.

But she had not yet
painted Bonito.

In her lifetime Frida Kahlo created more than 100 paintings.

Fifty-five are self-portraits,
which means they are paintings
that Frida made of herself.

Frida painted herself
with one of her hairless dogs.

She painted herself with
the monkeys, a cat,
and some of the birds, too.

When was she going to
paint Bonito?

Frida promised Bonito that
she would paint him someday.

So Bonito showed Frida
just how special he was!

Bonito started performing tricks for Frida and Diego.

He twirled.
He sang.
He danced
to music.

He even made kissing sounds!

Visitors at Frida's home
were happy to watch Bonito.

As a reward,
Bonito sometimes got
a little piece of butter.

Soon, the time came for Frida
to paint him!

Self-Portrait with Bonito became one of Frida Kahlo's most famous paintings. Bonito and Frida, and the bond they shared, were captured forever!

· Facts About Amazon Parrots ·

• Bonito came from a group of species called Amazon parrots. They are native to South America, Central America, and the Caribbean.
• Amazon parrots like to eat seeds, nuts, fruits, and vegetables. Butter actually isn't good for them.
• Many parrot species are endangered because people are cutting down forests and destroying the parrots' homes. Too many people are also collecting the parrots as pets.
• Humans have taste buds on their tongues, but Amazon parrots have taste buds on the roofs of their mouths.
• Amazon parrots are some of the best talkers among the more than 350 species of parrots.

· Facts About Frida Kahlo ·

• Frida Kahlo was born on June 6, 1907, and died on July 13, 1954.
• Frida originally wanted to become a doctor.
• She started painting after she got into a bus accident and wanted something to do while she recovered.
• Frida's husband was Diego Rivera, an artist most famous for his murals.
• Frida's home, la Casa Azul, is now the Frida Kahlo Museum.